DATE DUE		
		DISCARD		

HOLOCAUST BIOGRAPHIES

Anne Frank
Young Voice of the Holocaust

Magdalena Alagna

THE ROSEN PUBLISHING GROUP, INC.
NEW YORK

Published in 2001 by The Rosen Publishing Group, Inc.
29 East 21st Street, New York, NY 10010

First Edition

Library of Congress Cataloging-in-Publication Data

Alagna, Magdalena.
Anne Frank : young voice of the Holocaust / by
Magdalena Alagna.
p. cm. — (Holocaust biographies)
Includes bibliographical references and index.
ISBN 0-8239-3373-3
1. Frank, Anne, 1929–1945—Juvenile literature. 2. Jewish
children in the Holocaust—Netherlands—Amsterdam—
Biography—Juvenile literature. 3. Jews—Netherlands —
Amsterdam—Biography—Juvenile literature. 4. Amsterdam
(Netherlands)—Biography—Juvenile literature. 5. Frank,
Anne, 1929–1945. Achterhuis. [1. Frank, Anne, 1929–1945.
2. Jews—Netherlands—Biography. 3. Holocaust, Jewish
(1939–1945)] I. Title. II. Series.
DS135.N6 F7314 2001
940.53'18'092—dc21

2001000688

Contents

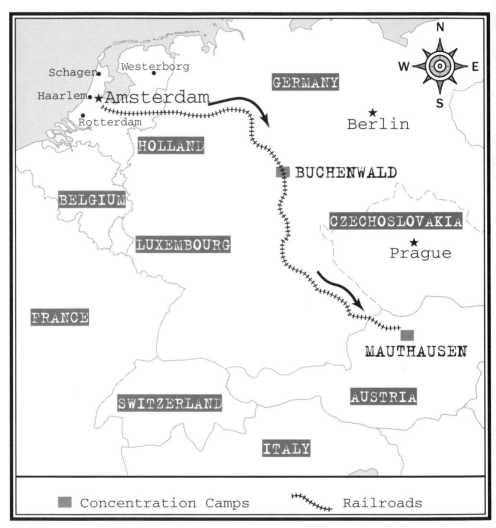

This map shows the route that Nazi trains took to transport Jewish deportees from Amsterdam to the concentration camps of Buchenwald and Mauthausen during the SS raids in 1941.

Introduction: Testimony of the Human Spirit

In one of Anne Frank's last diary entries, she wrote, "It's really a wonder that I haven't dropped all my ideals, because they seem so absurd and impossible to carry out. Yet I keep them, because in spite of everything, I still believe that people are really good at heart."

Anne Frank's hopeful and courageous spirit has been an inspiration to millions of people. Through her famous diary, Anne's words will live on forever. *Anne Frank: The Diary of a Young Girl* is one of the most widely read books throughout the world. It is so popular that it has been translated into more than fifty languages.

Anne Frank was a victim in one of the greatest crimes against humanity that the world has ever seen: the Holocaust. The Holocaust was the mass killing of the Jewish people in Germany and in countries occupied by German forces during World War II. The Nazis forced the Jews into places called concentration camps. The conditions in these camps were terrible. Many people were murdered and others were subject to starvation and torture. Anne Frank only survived a few months in the Nazi concentration camps, but her words live on.

Anne Frank is remembered because of the diary that she began keeping in 1942, three days after receiving the journal from her parents for her thirteenth birthday. Anne wrote her first diary entry just three weeks before the family was forced to go into hiding. She kept the diary for two years, until August 1944, when Anne and the other seven people in hiding were arrested by the Nazis. Their only "crime" was being Jewish.

In Hiding

Otto Frank, Anne's father, made a hiding place in the annex of his company, located at 263

Prinsengracht in Amsterdam, Holland. Anne Frank and her mother, father, sister, and four others lived together in the small, cramped annex for two years.

Anne Frank was thirteen years old when she went into hiding. She dealt with all of the ordinary problems that teenagers face—all of the confusing thoughts and emotions—and she did this under extraordinary conditions. Anne described in her diary what it was like to live in the small annex with so many others. Not only did they have very little privacy, but they had to live with the constant fear of discovery. They knew that if they were found they might be killed.

The Diary

Anne Frank was an unusual young woman for her time. During the 1940s, girls were not expected to have a life outside of home and family. Many girls have such goals for themselves today, but during the 1940s it was

The Anne Frank House (*center*) at 263 Prinsengracht in
Amsterdam, where she hid for two years.

not so common. Anne wrote about these feelings in her diary: "I want to go further, I can't imagine having to live like Mummy . . . I must have something more than a husband and children, something I can devote myself to."

Anne longed to be recognized for her writing and hoped to be a great writer. Her diary, published after her death, assured her a place in history. She addressed her diary as "Kitty" and looked upon it as the friend to whom she could confide all of her thoughts and feelings. Of course, Anne Frank often was unhappy, given her circumstances, but she also wrote in her diary about the experiences that gave her joy.

Anne Frank observed the world around her and wrote about what she thought and how she felt. She looked inside herself for strength and for the motivation to continue in the world without despair. This isn't easy for anyone to do, and it wasn't easy for Anne Frank, either. She wrote about how the people living in the annex got on one another's nerves and how she lost her temper with them.

One of the truly incredible stories in the diary is the account of how Anne's feelings of friendship for her friend Peter, who lived in the secret annex with Anne and her family, blossomed into love. Anne's love for Peter is an amazing example of how tender feelings can bloom even during a dark and frightening time. Anne found a source of inspiration and power in her love for Peter, even though it became clear to her that she could not rely on him to be all that she wanted him to be.

Anne Frank's story is an inspiration because her writing stands as a bright spot alongside the tragedy of the Holocaust. Her diary reflects the testimony of the human spirit, which at its best, can look past its present hardships and cling to a belief in a good life. Anne wrote: "It's utterly impossible for me to build my life on a foundation of chaos, suffering and death. I see the world being slowly transformed into a wilderness, I hear the approaching thunder that, one day, will destroy us too, I feel the suffering of millions. And yet, when I look up at the sky, I somehow feel that everything will change for the better, that this cruelty too will end, that peace and tranquility will return once more."

1. Anne's Story

In recounting Anne Frank's story, the natural place to start is with her parents, Otto and Edith Frank. We have vivid descriptions of them, which Anne wrote in her diary, and some of the descriptions are quite harsh. In this chapter you'll get an impartial view of the Franks.

Otto Frank was born in Frankfurt am Main, Germany, in 1889. Otto's father, Michael Frank, owned and managed a bank in Frankfurt until his death in 1909. After Michael Frank's death, his wife managed the family bank. As a young man, Otto was not too thrilled about joining the banking business, but he did eventually work in the family bank, until it closed in 1933.

Otto served in the German army during World War I and attained the rank of lieutenant. Otto Frank married Edith Holländer in 1925. Edith had been born in Germany, too—in Aachen. They settled in Frankfurt to begin raising a family. Like many Jews during that time period, the Franks identified themselves as German citizens. Although the rumblings of Nazi propaganda against the Jews were first starting to be heard, the Nazis were not yet in power in Germany.

Anne Is Born

Annelies Marie Frank was born on June 12, 1929, in Frankfurt am Main, Germany. She was the second child of Otto and Edith Frank. Her sister, Margot, was three years older. Although her full name was Annelies, the family called her Anne.

The Frank family was not exactly wealthy, but they were a well-to-do family. Otto Frank, after the family bank closed, became a partner in a business that made pectin, which is an ingredient in jam. His business allowed him many opportunities to travel all over the world. He traveled frequently to Amsterdam, Holland, on business.

The Political Situation in Germany During Anne's Early Childhood

At the time that Adolf Hitler was coming to power in Germany, it was the time of the Great Depression in the United States. During the early years of the Nazi regime, many German Jews felt, in spite of the Nazis, that they didn't want to leave the homes, the businesses, and the lives that they had made in Germany. They had no idea how bad things eventually would become for Jews in Germany and in other parts of Europe.

Many countries were not eager to accept Jewish refugees. The economy was not only depressed in the United States—much of the world was grappling with economic crisis. Countries feared that to have refugees looking for jobs made work scarcer for citizens. Also, Jews emigrating from Germany were allowed to take very little money with them. Many countries did not want to accept refugees who were so poor.

In 1933, Hitler became the chancellor of Germany. That means he had total political power. The Germans called him the Führer, which means "leader" in German.

Moving to Amsterdam

In 1933, in response to Hitler's anti-Jewish laws, Otto Frank opened a branch of his business in Amsterdam, Holland, and started to make arrangements to move his family there. While he was in Amsterdam making the arrangements, the rest of the Frank family stayed in Frankfurt with Otto's and Edith's mothers for a while. The Frank family moved to a house in Amsterdam in 1933, when Anne was four years old.

There were several Jewish families that had emigrated from Germany to Amsterdam; among them were Hanneli "Lies" Goslar's family. Hanneli, or Hannah, was one of Anne's closest friends throughout her life. The van Pels family, who later went into hiding with the Frank family, also lived nearby in Amsterdam.

Anne's Girlhood in Amsterdam

Anne and Hannah started in a Montessori school not long after arriving in Amsterdam. A Montessori school is a special type of school, named after Maria Montessori, the woman who created this particular system of education. In a Montessori school, studies are geared to enhance the special interests and talents of each individual child. The little German girls not only had to go to a new school, they also had to learn a whole new language—Dutch. Anne did well in school and was popular with both boys and girls. She had a lot of friends.

Portrait of Anne Frank at her desk in school

Anne later wrote of her girlhood before she went into hiding, "Yes, it was heavenly. Five admirers on every street corner, twenty or so friends, the favorite of most of my teachers, spoiled rotten by father and mother, bags full of candy and a big allowance. What more could anyone ask for?"

Making Plans to Hide in the Annex

In September of 1939, World War II began when the German army invaded Poland. The Nazis invaded and occupied the Netherlands in 1940. The same kinds of anti-Semitic laws were beginning to be enforced in Amsterdam as were already being enforced in Germany.

In 1940, Otto Frank established a wholesale business in herbs and spices on the Prinsengracht location. The annex of the Prinsengracht building would become the famous annex Anne wrote about in her diary.

What exactly is an annex? In Amsterdam in those days, houses were built long and narrow. Usually two houses were built close to each other, one behind the other, with a courtyard and an annex, or an extra set of rooms, in between.

Miep Gies was one of Otto Frank's employees in the business on Prinsengracht. She helped Otto Frank move many belongings, including clothes, books, furniture, and food, into the annex for a full year before the family had to go into hiding.

The Nazi Persecution of the Jews

By 1942, the second year of the German occupation of the Netherlands, it became clear that the situation for Jews under Nazi rule was only going to worsen. On June 20, 1942, Anne wrote: "Anti-Jewish decrees followed each other in quick succession. Jews must wear a yellow star, Jews must hand in their bicycles,

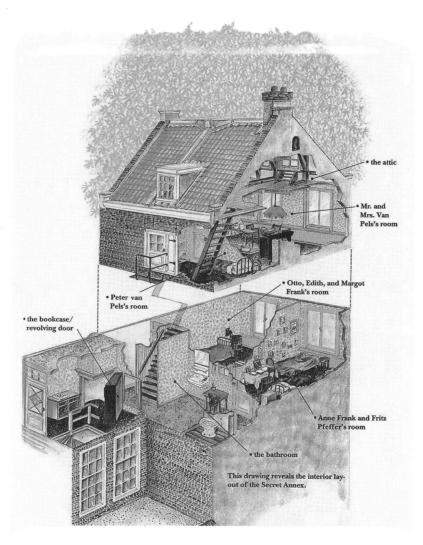

the attic

Mr. and Mrs. Van Pels's room

Otto, Edith, and Margot Frank's room

Peter van Pels's room

the bookcase/ revolving door

Anne Frank and Fritz Pfeffer's room

the bathroom

This drawing reveals the interior layout of the Secret Annex.

A cross-section view of the house where Anne Frank and her family hid is shown in this diagram.

Jews are banned from trams and are forbidden to drive. Jews must be indoors by eight o'clock and cannot even sit in their own gardens after that hour. Jews may not take part in public sports. Jews may not visit Christians. Our freedom was strictly limited."

The yellow star that Anne wrote about was the Star of David, which is an important and holy symbol in the Jewish religion. Also, Jews had to have a "J" stamped on their passports, for "Jew." Jews could only shop in Jewish stores and only between the hours of three and five in the afternoon. In addition, Jewish schoolchildren had to leave their schools and go to all-Jewish, college preparatory schools.

Hannah Goslar described this time in the documentary film *Anne Frank Remembered*: "It was scary. You would go to school, and your classmates would just disappear. If you didn't see someone in school, you just had to hope that they were sick and that something more terrible hadn't happened to them. Out of fifty students in my class at the beginning of the term, I was the only one to be present for the graduation examination at the end of the year."

Margot Receives a Letter

In July 1942, Margot Frank received a letter telling her to report to a labor camp. At that time, many people didn't know exactly what

Jewish students are humiliated before their classmates. The inscription on the blackboard reads "The Jew is our greatest enemy! Beware of the Jew!"

happened in those camps. This is, in part, because distinctions were made between the different kinds of concentration camps: labor camp, extermination camp, death camp, and transit camp. Also, many people could not believe that such terrible rumors of people being gassed could be true. Otto Frank took the letter to Margot as a sign that the whole family needed to go into hiding.

Hannah Goslar also recalled in *Anne Frank Remembered* that she had no idea of the Frank family's plan, even though Anne was her best friend. When the Franks fled to the annex, they left false clues in their abandoned apartment to suggest that they had gone to Switzerland, where Otto Frank's mother lived. They did this in the hope that the Nazis would give up looking for them. Hannah Goslar thought that her friend Anne was in Switzerland until the time that both of the girls were in a concentration camp, and Hannah heard, through a barbed wire fence, that Anne was on the other side of the fence.

2. Anne's Experience

It is not possible to understand Anne Frank's story without first understanding a little bit about the Nazi Party and how its anti-Semitic views launched one of the most organized and frightening campaigns of genocide the world has ever seen.

Some Germans were unhappy with the circumstances in Germany at the end of World War I. These Germans joined Adolf Hitler's new National Socialist German Workers' Party in 1923. The Nazi Party, as it was called, continued to gain popular support throughout the 1920s. Adolf Hitler became chancellor of Germany in 1933.

Hitler was an anti-Semite. He believed that Jews could be blamed for much of what was wrong in Germany and in the world. This is called scapegoating. Hitler's plan to make a stronger Germany was simple, yet terrifying: The plan called for controlling the Jews. It started with laws restricting their freedom and ended by depriving millions of Jews of their lives.

World War II

The German army invaded Poland in 1939, officially starting World War II. Great Britain and France declared war on Germany because Germany had invaded Poland. By 1940, Germany had invaded Denmark, Norway, Belgium, the Netherlands, and France. By 1941, Germany had invaded the Soviet Union, even though it had signed a pact with the Soviets promising not to attack.

In the winter of 1941–1942, the Soviets defeated the Germans at Stalingrad (now called Volgograd), in Russia. It was a turning point in the war. But Germany's ally, Japan, attacked the Americans stationed at Pearl

Harbor, Hawaii, on December 7, 1941, bringing the United States into the war.

During the first two years of the war, death camps and labor camps were built, and the first stages of the Holocaust were begun. The difference between death camps and labor camps was that the labor camps, or work camps, often did not have the facilities for mass killings that the death camps had.

The idea for the death camps came only after the Nazis had invaded Russia and had slaughtered every Jew that came within range of Nazi gunfire. Hitler decided that a more efficient method of extermination was needed. He didn't want his army to be distracted from the important tasks of invading and conquering countries. Poison gas chambers, disguised as showers, were devised, and the death camps were created.

There has been much written about whether people knew that Jews were being exterminated. After the war, many people claimed that the reports they heard about the killings were so incredible that they simply couldn't believe them.

Many people also wonder whether the Jews knew the extent of the danger. Several of the women interviewed in *Anne Frank Remembered* said that when they were in the concentration camps, they could see smoke from the furnaces that were used to rid the camps of many of the corpses. They could smell human flesh burning.

The Holocaust

The Holocaust is the name for the genocide of the Jews under Nazi rule. The Holocaust began with the herding of many Jews into ghettos—special sections of a city where ethnic groups lived. Often, ghettos had walls with gates that could be locked at night so inhabitants had to obey a curfew.

The next stage of the Holocaust was called the time of the Final Solution. The Final Solution meant mass killings or extermination of the Jews. By 1942, Hitler and the Nazis had figured out the most efficient way to do this. They transported the Jews from the German-occupied territories to death camps.

Going into Hiding

The Frank family went into hiding on July 6, 1942. Their neighbors, Herman and Auguste

A barbed wire fence separates the Waterlooplein market in the Jewish quarter from the rest of Amsterdam.

van Pels and their son Peter, joined them one week later. Mr. van Pels was Otto Frank's business partner. Later, Fritz Pfeffer joined the group in hiding.

Anne had code names for everyone she wrote about in the diary. She wrote of herself as Anne Robin. Margot, Otto, and Edith Frank were Betty, Frederik, and Nora Robin, respectively, although by the time the diary came into publication, Otto Frank had decided to keep the real names of the Frank family. Originally, the van Pels were called the van Daans, and Fritz Pfeffer was called Albert Dussel. Miep Gies was the only one whose real name appeared in the diary.

The Franks moved into the secret annex by traveling there on bicycles and on foot. They were able to take very few possessions with them. They entered through the front door of the warehouse. The secret bookcase entrance had not yet been built. It would not be built until August.

Helpers

Mr. Voskuijl, one of the men who worked in the warehouse with Otto Frank, helped them by building a bookcase to disguise the entrance to the annex. Mr. Voskuijl's daughter, Elizabeth "Bep" Voskuijl, worked as a secretary in Otto Frank's business, Gies & Co., and she also was a great help to the hideaways.

Miep Gies and her husband, Jan Gies, also worked in the warehouse with Otto Frank. Miep was the one who had the difficult task of getting Margot to the annex. Margot arrived there before the rest of her family.

Daily Routine in the Annex

What was life like in the secret annex? Everyone had to be extremely quiet for fear of being discovered. They were hiding in rooms above a business. That meant that they had to be especially quiet during the

The entrance to the secret annex had a staircase
hidden behind a bookcase.

workday hours, and even on weekends, when any noise would draw the most attention, coming from a building that was supposed to be empty. For hours at a time, they couldn't even flush the toilet because it would make too much noise.

Anything could lead to their discovery. There were many close calls during the two years that the eight hideaways lived in the annex. Someone on the street might notice a window left open just a crack and could jump to the conclusion that Jews were hiding on the top floor of the warehouse, and all would be lost.

Those in the annex tried to lead as much of a normal life as possible. For Anne, Margot, and Peter that meant studying and schoolwork. Anne's favorite subject was history, but she hated math. Anne counted among her hobbies reading about Greek and Roman mythology, and reading the genealogy of several European royal families, including the British royal family. She also liked to read

Anne Frank decorated her room with pictures of film stars and picture postcards.

movie magazines and eagerly followed the lives of movie stars. She collected postcards of the stars.

Anne, Margot, and Peter took courses in Latin and in shorthand. Shorthand is a system of notation used to write down a letter that someone dictates, or speaks, to his or her secretary. They also took correspondence courses that were completed through the mail.

Miep and Bep helped them by bringing their mail. Sometimes Anne and Margot helped Bep and Miep with tasks that could be done in the annex, such as filling paper packets with powdered gravy, a product of Gies & Co. Margot and Anne also helped with office work, such as filing. Anne wrote: "Bep's been giving Margot and me a lot of office work to do. It makes us both feel important, and it's a big help to her."

The residents of the annex woke up around 6:45 AM. By 8:30, they had to keep quiet because the workers were arriving in the warehouse below. At around 9:00 AM, they had their breakfast. After breakfast, they could barely move around or talk at all, because it was prime working hours for those in the warehouse.

By 12:30 PM, the warehouse was closed for lunch. The people in the annex also ate lunch then and listened to the BBC broadcast on the radio. At 2:00 PM, the warehouse was again open. From that time until 5:30 PM, when the warehouse was closed for the day, they mainly rested and read. By 9:00 PM, they started preparing for bed.

There were daily household chores, including food preparation. Everyone helped to peel potatoes; at one time, there were 230 pounds of them in the warehouse!

Bep Voskuijl received extra food from the grocer, which she then gave to the people in the annex. What was the food like in the annex? They went through "food cycles," which were periods of time during which there was only one kind of vegetable to eat. For instance, when only cabbage was available, they would eat sauerkraut three times a day, prepared in every possible way: with potatoes, with beans, and in soup. Sometimes there were no vegetables at all, or many of the vegetables were rotten. Anne sometimes had to rub beans with a cloth to get mold off of them.

Personal Relationships in the Annex

Anne had strong emotions and she did not always get along with everyone in the annex. She sometimes had a stormy relationship with the van Pels. According to Anne's diary entries, Mr. and Mrs. van Pels felt that Anne was in need of discipline, because Mrs. Frank was often too depressed to discipline Anne. During these times, Anne couldn't control her temper and she let everyone know exactly how she felt.

Anne shared a room with Fritz Pfeffer, who was forty years older than Anne. They irritated one another, which was understandable, considering the age and gender differences. Anne gave Pfeffer the code name Albert Dussel. *Dussel* means "mutt" in German!

Frequently, Anne was upset with one or another of the adults. She wrote on January 30, 1943: "They mustn't know my despair. I can't let them see the wound which they have caused. The whole day I hear nothing else but that I am an insufferable baby, and although I laugh about it and pretend not to take any notice, I do mind. I've got the nature that has been given to me and I'm sure it can't be bad."

Anne's Relationship with Peter

Anne had a special relationship with Peter van Pels. He was a few years older than she. They had been neighbors in Amsterdam before they went into hiding. Anne wrote in her diary that Peter told her how he remembered her in Amsterdam: surrounded by friends, always with one or two boys in the group, always laughing, and always the center of attention. Once they were in hiding, Peter and Anne spent a lot of time together in close quarters.

There came a time when Annie realized she had fallen in love with Peter. Peter was a sensitive young boy, reaching out for understanding in the same way that Anne was. Her feelings of love were so deep that she managed to feel truly happy, despite the conditions under which she was living.

It becomes clear while reading passages in Anne's diary that Peter was bound to be a disappointment to her. Peter was more responsive to Anne than any of the others, certainly more so than the adults. But in the long run, he was unable to fulfill Anne's needs. Anne was a very intellectual girl, a girl who wanted to be—who was—a writer, and Peter was not fond of book learning. He couldn't keep up with Anne's intellectual interests. Anne wrote on July 15, 1944: "I created an image of him in my mind. I needed a living person to whom I could pour out my heart; I wanted a friend who'd help to put me on the right road. I achieved what I wanted."

Eventually, she realized that she "had conquered Peter instead of he conquering her," and instead of him being a source of support for her, it was, in fact, the other way around. She wrote in the diary: "Now he clings to me, and for the time being, I don't see any way of shaking him off and putting him on his own feet. When I realized that he could not be a friend for my understanding, I thought I would at least try to lift him up of his narrow mindedness and make him do something with his youth."

Writing About Peter

Anne had a dream about a childhood love, named Peter. She realized that this dream represented her desire for a boyfriend. Not long after the dream, Anne realized that her thoughts had turned to Peter van Pels. She began to get a little more excited and happy whenever they were together.

Still, she wrote on February 18, 1944, "Don't think I'm in love, because I'm not, but I do have the feeling that something beautiful is going to develop between Peter and me, a kind of special friendship and a feeling of trust."

After working through complicated feelings of love for Peter, Anne wrote on July 15, 1944: "I created an image of him in my mind, pictured him as a quiet, sweet, sensitive boy badly in need of friendship and love! . . . When I finally got him to be my friend, it automatically developed into an intimacy that, when I think about it now, seems outrageous . . . Our time together leaves him feeling satisfied, but just makes me want to start all over again . . . I soon realized he could never be a kindred spirit . . ."

Anne's Relationship with Her Family

Often, Anne did not get along well with her mother. In one of her diary entries, Anne describes her mother's "cold, mocking ways," and maintains that she, Anne, had to mother herself. Anne frequently got upset when she felt that the adults were treating her like a child. She wanted to be looked upon as the mature and capable young woman that she thought she was.

Although her father annoyed her sometimes, Anne still admired him and wanted to grow up

The last family photo taken of Anne Frank with her sister Margot and parents in Merwedeplein. The photo was sent to cousins in Switzerland in May, 1940.

to be like him. Otto Frank was every girl's dream dad. Anne adored him and identified more with him than she did with Edith Frank or her sister Margot, who was a quiet, ladylike, studious girl. Anne definitely was her daddy's little girl. Anne frequently wrote in her diary that the situation would have been unbearable in the annex if it were not for her father, who often took her part in arguments.

She describes in the diary that part of the process of growing into adulthood was realizing that there were some things for which she couldn't rely on her beloved father. The only one who could be counted on to cherish Anne's innermost self was Anne herself—and Kitty.

Anne had a touch-and-go relationship with Margot. Anne seemed to find it difficult sometimes to be close to a sister who was "such a goody-goody." However, the two sisters shared some heart-to-heart talks in the annex and sometimes wrote each other notes just for fun. Later, they would be inseparable in the concentration camps.

Anne *(center)* and sister Margot sitting on their
father's lap

Anne's Relationship with Miep: A Special Bond of Understanding

Miep Gies was the only person who was mentioned by name in Anne's diary. Miep felt that she and Anne shared a special relationship, a closeness that was not understood by the others in the annex.

"Anne was a very special girl," Miep Gies said in *Anne Frank Remembered*. "When I got to the annex every day, many of the people, Mrs. Frank especially, would be worried and nervous. But Anne would meet me at the door right away, cheerful and eager to talk of news from the outside."

3. The Story of the Diary

Although Anne Frank's story was adapted for the stage and the screen, and though it has been the subject of many books and articles, no one tells Anne's story as well as Anne herself. It is only through reading Anne's diary that one gets the full drama of her story.

When the family was going into hiding, they couldn't take many of their possessions with them, and they couldn't be seen strolling out of their house with suitcases. How would they smuggle their clothes and belongings into the secret annex?

In Anne's diary entry of July 8, 1942, she described their flight: "The four of us were wrapped in so many layers of clothes it looked as if we were going off to spend the night in a refrigerator, and all that just so we could take more clothes with us. No Jew in our situation would dare leave the house with a suitcase full of clothes. I was wearing two undershirts, three pairs of underpants, a dress, and over that a skirt, a jacket, a raincoat, two pairs of stockings, heavy shoes, a cap, a scarf, and lots more. I was suffocating even before we left the house . . . "

Kitty

The first entry in Anne's diary is dated June 14, 1942, two days after her thirteenth birthday and three weeks before she and her family went into hiding. She wrote, "I hope I will be able to confide everything to you, as I have never been able to confide in anyone, and I hope you will be a great source of comfort and support."

Anne called her diary Kitty, a name which, Hannah Goslar has said in interviews, was the name of one of the characters in a series of novels that were popular with the young women of that time. Anne named her diary so that she would feel as if she were writing letters to a friend, instead of just writing down the facts of her life.

At first, Annie's main purpose of keeping a diary was so that she would have a confidant. She wrote: "Writing in a diary is a really strange experience for someone like me. Not only because I've never written anything before, but also because it seems to me that later on neither I nor anyone else will be interested in the musings of a thirteen-year-old school girl." How wrong she was!

Anne Frank's diary has served as the testimony of one person's experience of the Holocaust. But it also serves as a reminder to future generations of two important things: the courage and dignity of the human spirit, as well as the capacity for evil in every human being as evidenced by the actions of the Nazis during World War II.

The first few entries show that Anne was a typical young girl; concerned with boys and her popularity. After the Frank family went into hiding, Anne wrote about the life that she and the others led in the annex.

When she had filled up the original diary she'd received for her birthday, Miep Gies and Bep Voskuijl brought her business ledgers and even loose sheets of paper to continue writing. Anne kept those in one of Mr. Frank's suitcases.

Anne's Many Emotions

Anne spared no detail in describing her despair. Many entries had to do with how the adults in the annex were driving her up the wall. But Anne wasn't just critical of others. She was able to analyze herself as well. In one of the entries, she wrote: "In everything I do, I can watch myself as if I were a stranger. I can stand across from the everyday Anne and, without being biased or making excuses, watch what she's doing, both the good and the bad."

Of course, living under such conditions, especially with the constant fear of discovery, meant that Anne was often gloomy. On February 3, 1944, she wrote: "I've reached the point where I hardly care whether I live or die. The world will keep on turning without me, and I can't do anything to change events anyway. I'll just let matters take their course and concentrate on studying and hope that everything will be all right in the end."

However, there are also many entries in which Anne talked optimistically about her hopes and plans for the future. Just the writing of the diary itself gave her much joy. She wrote, "When I write, I can shake off all my cares."

She also wrote on May 3, 1944, after more than a year in hiding, "I'm blessed with many things: happiness, a cheerful disposition, and strength. Every day I feel myself maturing, I feel liberation drawing near, I feel the beauty of nature and the goodness of the people around me. Every day I think what a fascinating and amusing adventure this is! With all that, why should I despair?"

Making Sense of the War

In her diary, Anne tried to make sense of the war and what was going on in Holland and the world. The only news she had to go on were the reports the family listened to on the radio. She wrote of the deportations on October 9, 1942: "Our many Jewish friends and acquaintances are being taken away in droves. The Gestapo is treating them very roughly and transporting them in cattle cars to Westerbork, the big camp in Drenthe to which they're sending all the Jews . . . If it's that bad in Holland, what must it be like in those faraway and uncivilized places where the Germans are sending them? We assume that most of them are being murdered. The English radio says they're being gassed."

She also tried to figure out what was going on in the annex among its residents, and, most

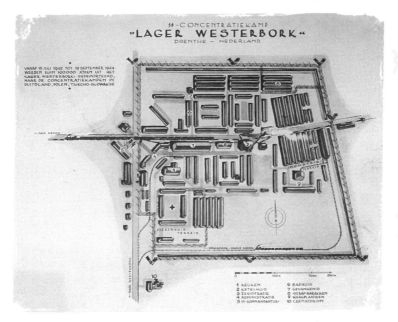

A map of the Westerbork transit camp is pictured here. Until July 1942, it was a refugee camp for Jews who had moved illegally to the Netherlands.

important, what was going on inside of herself. She admitted in her diary that many of her feelings contradicted each other, and though she tried to employ reason, she often couldn't make sense of the way she felt. One thing she was sure of: She dreamed of becoming a writer so that she would be remembered after her death.

The Call for Diaries

In 1944, the Dutch government, which had been in exile in London for most of the time that the Germans occupied Holland, broadcast a request over the BBC, the radio station from London, that people should save their wartime diaries. Anne wrote of hearing the broadcast: "Mr. Bolkestein, the Cabinet Minister, speaking on the Dutch broadcast from London, said that after the war a collection would be made of diaries and letters dealing with the war. Of course, everyone pounced on my diary."

After hearing this, Anne began to rewrite the diary with the intent of publishing it after the war. She rewrote more than 300 pages in just a few months.

Close Calls

Some of the events recorded in Anne's diary were accounts of things that could have put everyone in danger. As one reads through the diary, one can experience somewhat the terrible feeling of suspense that must have been felt constantly by those in the annex—and that's just from reading about some of the close calls they had.

For instance, in March 1943, at about eight at night, two boys climbed into the warehouse to see what they could find there. Peter van Pels heard a barrel fall, and he and Mr. Frank heard two door slams. The boys had heard a toilet flush and ran out of the warehouse, probably with some spices they'd stolen. The boys didn't tell anyone about this for years.

The warehouse also was robbed several times. The last time it was robbed, in April 1944, some of the annex men went downstairs to scare away the intruder. One of the night watchmen saw the men and alerted the police. A policeman made a tour of the warehouse, and even rattled the bookcase behind which was the entrance to the secret annex, but those hiding there were not discovered at that time.

Mr. van Maaren

Although the people living in the annex had a few helpers who worked in the warehouse, there were staff changes that could have affected their safety. Mr. Voskuijl was taken ill and was replaced by Mr. van Maaren.

Mr. van Maaren was suspicious about the annex. In April 1944, as a trap, he started to put things such as books, pencils, and papers on the edges of tables and other furniture in the warehouse. He also began to sprinkle flour on the floor before he left at night. Then, when the people in the annex came downstairs into the warehouse, they knocked the pencils off the tables and left footprints in the flour. Fortunately, the helpers in the warehouse were able to warn those in the annex to be more careful about such things.

The End of Life in Hiding

On August 4, 1944, the police raided the annex after receiving an anonymous phone tip. Someone must have suspected, or knew about the Franks and others hiding in the annex at 263 Prinsengracht, but it was never discovered who betrayed them to the police. Rewards were given to people who betrayed Jews in hiding: one week's pay for betraying five Jews. Many people during wartime wanted the extra money they could get for turning in Jews.

The SS—the *Schutzstaffel,* or guard unit of the Nazi Party—came tramping through the apartment and arrested all eight of its occupants. One of the soldiers shook Anne's diary out of the suitcase it was in. He needed the suitcase to carry some of the valuables he was going to confiscate. It is amazing that the SS soldier did not take the diary, too. The Nazis were in the habit of taking people's letters and diaries.

4. The Beginning of the End

When the residents of the annex were arrested by the SS on August 4, 1944, they were taken to the train station, loaded onto cattle cars, and taken to Westerbork. Westerbork was a transit camp, a place where the Nazis collected large numbers of Jews who had been deported from their home countries and who were destined for extermination camps such as Auschwitz. Westerbork was the transit camp where Dutch Jews were sent.

In the book *The Last Seven Months of Anne Frank* by Willy Lindwer, several women who had befriended Anne and Margot in the concentration camps of Auschwitz and

Bergen-Belsen said that they remembered seeing the Frank family standing together on the train platform, waiting for the train that would take them to Westerbork. They remembered that the family was wearing sport clothes and carrying backpacks. They looked as though they were ready to go on a vacation, except for the fact that they were so pale.

The train ride from Westerbork to Auschwitz was long and uncomfortable; it took two or three days to get there. So many people were crowded into the cattle cars that there was no way anyone could sit down or rest. There was also very little food to go around. The cattle cars were filthy; there were no bathrooms on the train.

Auschwitz

When the prisoners got off the train at Auschwitz, they saw the sign arched over the entrance to the camp: *Arbeit Macht Frei:* "Work Will Make You Free." The bright spotlights on tall poles that were at the entrance to the camp threw an eerie gray-white light over everything.

Survivors of Auschwitz have said in interviews that the Nazis moved among the Jews, stealing any valuables the Jews might have brought with them. Many of the prisoners crushed things such as wedding

A crate full of rings confiscated from prisoners in the Buchenwald concentration camp

rings into the ground, rather than let them fall into the hands of the Nazis.

The prisoners were immediately subjected to a selection process. People were selected either for death—these Jews went directly to the gas chambers, which were disguised as showers—or they were picked for work. Most of the children, especially those under the age of fifteen, were marked for immediate death. Anyone who looked sick or old or as if he or she wouldn't make a good worker also went directly to the gas chambers.

Some people were selected for medical experiments. Dr. Joseph Mengele, a high-ranking Nazi official, ran these experiments, where people were treated in unimaginable, horrific ways.

The Frank family was separated at Auschwitz. Like the other Jews who arrived before them, the Franks were separated by gender. Otto Frank never saw any member of his family again. Edith, Margot, and Anne were taken to the women's barracks. There they were stripped of their clothes and given rags to wear. The Nazis also checked in the Jews' mouths for gold fillings, which were removed to help pay for the war. The women's heads were shaved. Anne cried to see her long hair shaved off; it was her favorite feature about herself. Then numbers were tattooed on their arms.

Hungarian Jewish women selected for work march toward the camp in Auschwitz after being disinfected and having their heads shaved.

Roll Call

Among the many horrifying experiences at Auschwitz was the daily roll call, which could last for hours. Sometimes it lasted all through the night. Inmates had to line up outside—even if it was freezing, raining, or snowing—wearing nothing but thin rags of clothing, if they were lucky enough to have clothes.

There were many rules about how the inmates should line up, such as standing at least one arm's length apart from each other, making it easier for the Nazis to count them. The prisoners of Auschwitz were careful to follow the rules, because if the count came out wrong, they would have to stand for hours and hours until the count came out right. Some people, weakened from starvation or illness, dropped dead while standing in line for roll call. That also threw off the count and made the roll call begin again.

Living Conditions

In addition to the meager food (one roll might have to last a person for more than a week, so people often tore the rolls up into little pieces so they would last longer), it was difficult, if not impossible, to get clean water. When there was water, so many people were crowded around trying to get at it that often many people didn't get any. Those who did couldn't be sure it was clean. It was safer to stick with coffee because it was boiled. Sometimes people used the coffee to rinse out their mouths, because there was no water with which to wash.

Because the camps were so crowded and so dirty, there was much illness. Sometimes people had trouble sleeping because they were crowded eight or ten to a bunk (there were three tiers of bunks in the barracks) and there were fleas everywhere.

The bodies of the dead were littered all around the camps. There were so many corpses that it was difficult to cremate or even to bury them all. It became a way of life for the inmates of the concentration camps to be stepping around piles of dead bodies.

Anne and Margot were in one of the bottom bunks, by the door. That was an unfortunate place to be because the wind whistled through the cracks in the door all night long, freezing the girls in their bunks. Once the prisoners were inside for the night, anyone who went outdoors was shot by the SS soldiers who stood guard throughout the night. That meant that if someone had to go to the latrine, which was located in another part of the camp, she couldn't.

The Work in the Camps

People counted themselves comparatively lucky if they were not chosen to go immediately to the gas chambers. The work in the camp was dirty, backbreaking, and meaningless. The Nazis wanted to break the spirit of the Jews by giving them difficult but pointless tasks to do. For instance, some people were ordered to move big, heavy rocks from one corner of the yard to another.

Anne had to break apart batteries. It is rumored that Otto Frank had tried to secure this job for her. Although it was dirty work (the carbon inside the batteries sprayed all over), and no one knew why they had to break apart these batteries, it was a relatively good job because it could be done indoors.

There were Jews at Auschwitz who had been in the camp for a long time, and some of them helped the Nazis patrol the other Jews. They probably would have been killed for refusing to do this. However, these people could be very mean to the prisoners. There are many interviews from women who remember these individuals hitting people, yelling at them when they didn't move fast enough at their tasks, and generally mistreating the other Jews.

Concentration camp inmates were forced to perform backbreaking labor.

Anne and Edith Frank in the Camps

Women who were in Auschwitz with Anne and Edith Frank have described in interviews the relationship between the women of the Frank family. We know from Anne's diary that she often did not get along well with her mother. Many teenage girls have fights with their parents while they are establishing their own identities. Anne was establishing her identity while she was in hiding. Due to the unfortunate and unusual circumstances, the normal tension that exists between parents and teens was greatly escalated for Anne and Edith Frank.

All of that seemed to have been forgotten in the concentration camps, though. The women clung to each other for support. In the face of such a devastating horror as Auschwitz, the petty squabbles between Anne and her mother in the past were unimportant.

Anne and Margot Frank, sick with scabies, which cause sores on the body, were transported to Bergen-Belsen on October 28, 1944. Edith Frank died of starvation in Auschwitz on January 6, 1945, one day before the camp was liberated.

Bergen-Belsen

Anne and Margot Frank were among the last people to be transported to Bergen-Belsen. The camp had not been designed to house as many people as were there at that time, so newcomers were put in tents that were pitched outside. Not too long after the arrival of these new prisoners, the tents in which they were put were blown down in a terrible storm. They were then crammed into the already overcrowded barracks.

Hannah Goslar described in *Anne Frank Remembered* how she found out that Anne and Margot were in Bergen-Belsen: "I heard a woman talking on the other side of the fence from me. It sounded like Mrs. van Pels." (Mrs. van Pels had also been Hanneli's neighbor as

well as Anne's in Amsterdam, so she knew
Mrs. van Pels's voice.) "I called out to her. She
said, 'I'll get Anne for you. I can't get Margot
because she is very sick and can't get up.'
Anne came to the fence. She started to cry,
and I started to cry."

Women, crowded three or more to a single bunk, were
forced to share the filthy, squalid barracks in the
concentration camps. These subhuman conditions led
to the spread of contagious diseases. These are the
survivors shortly after liberation.

"I had a little food saved. I tried to throw some food to Anne, over the fence, and I heard her cry out 'Oh, a woman standing next to me caught that food, and now she won't give it back!'"

Another of Anne's friends in Bergen-Belsen said that Anne might have held on a little longer after Margot died of typhus if she had known at the time that her father was still alive. Anne Frank died of typhus in Bergen-Belsen. She was just fifteen years old.

The Fate of the Other People in the Annex

Mr. van Pels was the first of the people in the annex to go to the gas chambers at Auschwitz. Mrs. van Pels was transported to several concentration camps. She did not survive, though it isn't recorded when and how she died. Peter van Pels was forced to take part in the death march from Auschwitz to Mauthausen, Austria. It is said that he died just three days before the camp was liberated. Fritz Pfeffer died in the Neuengamme concentration camp. Otto Frank was the only one of the people in the annex to survive the concentration camps. He was found alive in Auschwitz when it was liberated on January 7, 1945.

A death march from Dachau. The column of prisoners is surrounded by heavily armed guards.

The Beginning of the End

Death march is the name given to the forced evacuation of prisoners from concentration camps. When Germany surrendered, the Nazis made all of the inmates of the camps flee so that the Allies would find the camps deserted when they came to liberate them. Many people died on these marches from the physical hardship. The prisoners were made to march long hours without food and in the bitter cold. Many of them, weakened from months of starvation and illness in the camps, could not take the stress of the march. Others died at the hands of the Nazis, who shot anyone who could not keep up the pace of the march or who marched out of line.

5. Publishing the Diary and Short Stories

Miep Gies, who helped the Franks while they were in hiding, was not arrested. Miep and her husband Jan were members of the Dutch resistance. They helped many people during World War II.

After the Nazis had taken away everyone who had hidden in the annex, Miep, Jan, and two other helpers went back to the hiding place. It was then that they saw the scattered papers lying on the floor. They were afraid to stay there for too long, in case the Nazis came back. One week later, they returned to move the furniture, and Miep took the diary, notebooks, and all of the loose papers that were Anne's journals.

Jan and Miep Gies, coworkers of Otto Frank, were a
great help to Anne Frank and her family.

Miep did not read the diary. She put it in a drawer and didn't even look at it for almost a year. One of the reasons was because she thought the diary might include things that would get her in trouble with the Nazis if the Germans got their hands on it.

The Nazis had arrested some of the people who helped the Frank family, including the grocer who gave Bep Voskuijl more vegetables than Gies & Co.'s ration card allowed. The grocer had guessed correctly that Bep was aiding Jews in hiding. He was arrested by the Nazis and charged with the "crime" of helping the Jews.

After the war, Otto visited Miep and delivered the news of Anne's death. She gave the diary to Otto.

In an interview that she gave in 1995, Miep Gies said that every year on August 4, the day that her friends disappeared, she shuts her curtains and does not answer the door or her phone. "I have never overcome that shock," she said.

Typing Up the Diary

After Auschwitz was liberated, Otto Frank returned to Amsterdam by way of Russia. He began to type up Anne's diary and to translate it from Dutch into German. Otto wanted to show it to his mother, Anne's grandmother, who had escaped to Switzerland.

While she was still in hiding, Anne had rewritten much of the original diary, with the intention of giving it to the Dutch authorities after the war. She had begun to edit the text, leaving out certain parts that she thought might slow down the story. She also rewrote some things to make them more clear or interesting.

Otto used Anne's edited version as a guide for the version of the diary that he was typing. He edited the writing some more. He took out some parts because they included unflattering things about Edith Frank and about Anne's parents' marriage. Otto didn't want his wife to be remembered in a negative way after her death.

Otto also took out some of the writing about Anne's intimate thoughts and feelings. He thought some of those passages were not modest. Today, girls can express things more openly than they could at the time that Otto was typing up Anne's diary. Then, many things were considered improper for girls to discuss.

Once the manuscript was ready, Otto gave it to his friend to read. Eventually, Otto wanted to publish the diary. He thought it was an excellent way for readers to learn about the Nazis and what they did to the Jews. He was right. *Anne Frank: The Diary of a Young Girl* is required reading for most eighth-grade students in the United States. But some people haven't always felt that way about Anne's diary.

Trying to Get the Diary Published

At first, Otto Frank had a hard time finding a company to publish the book. Immediately after World War II, not many publishers wanted to print books about the Holocaust. Publishers thought the tragedy was still too fresh. People were still hurt. Too many had lost loved ones, many had lost everything. Publishers were convinced that the public did not want to read about the Holocaust.

One of Otto's friends passed along the diary to the historian Jan Romein to read. Jan Romein wrote about the diary in a daily newspaper called *Het Parool*. The article, translated as "A Child's Voice," was so touching that it gained the attention of the Contact Publishing Group, a Dutch publishing house.

The diary was first published in 1947, under the title *Het Achterhuis*, roughly translated as "The Secret Annex." It was published in the United States in 1952 as *Anne Frank: The Diary of a Young Girl*. About 30 percent of the diary was published at that time. The Contact Publishing Group was cautious. Editors agreed with Otto Frank about leaving out some of the parts about Anne's sexuality. They also agreed to leave out some of what Anne wrote about her mother and others in the annex who got on her nerves at times.

The original 1947 printing done by Contact was only 1,500 copies. So many people wanted to read the diary, however, that another edition was quickly printed. Within five years, there were German, French, and English versions of the book. Since that time, the diary has been translated into fifty-five languages. More than 24 million copies have been sold.

Later Editions of the Diary

In 1986, the Netherlands Institute for War Documentation published *The Critical Edition* of Anne's diary. This edition has all of the entries that Otto Frank and Contact Publishing Group left out of the first edition.

The entries that Anne rewrote after March 1944 are placed next to the original entries. The 1986 edition also includes information about the tests done to make sure the diary was authentic. It includes some of the short stories and sketches Anne wrote while she was in hiding, too.

In 1995, Doubleday published *The Definitive Edition* on the fiftieth anniversary of Anne Frank's death. This edition was based on a new English translation of the original Dutch text. It also includes the entries that Otto Frank and Contact Publishing Group left out of the original 1947 version of the book.

Controversy

Anne's diary became more and more famous, and so did the image of Anne Frank herself. To many people, she became the symbol of innocence in a dark period in history. That began to change as the diary was examined more closely, and especially as more material was added that originally was left out of the 1947 edition. Some of the material that was withheld showed that Anne was not a symbol of innocence—she was a very human young woman, capable of many moods and fancies and feelings, not all of them sweet, pure, and good.

In 1998, five pages that were never published before came to the attention of the public. The pages were found in the possession of a man, Cor Suijk, who said he got the pages from Otto Frank shortly before Otto's death in 1980. Cor Suijk said that Otto asked him not to try to get these pages published until after Otto Frank and his second wife had died. In 1998, Otto Frank's wife was still alive, but her daughter told Suijk that it was okay to publish the pages anyway. These pages contained some of the material about Anne's sexuality, as well as her complex relationship with her parents.

Doubts About the Diary's Authenticity

Neo-Nazi groups have often said that the diary of Anne Frank is not genuine. Neo-Nazis are people who agree with the ideas of the Nazi Party and would like to see the Nazi Party gain political power again.

These neo-Nazi groups would like to prove that the diary is not authentic, most likely because then they could try to cover up the horrific and barbaric activities of the Nazis during World War II. As long as there is testimony such as Anne Frank's diary, there is a witness and there is a voice to the horrors of the Holocaust, which no neo-Nazi group can deny.

Because of the accusations that the diary was a fake, Otto Frank had willed the original diaries to the Netherlands Institute for War Documentation. They received the diaries after Otto Frank's death.

The Netherlands Institute for War Documentation performed tests on the paper, ink, and glue used in the diary. These tests proved that the diary was written during the 1940s. Tests also were performed on Anne's handwriting. Samples from the diary were compared to Anne's other writings such as letters with stamp cancellations, which had dates on them. These tests proved beyond the shadow of a doubt that Anne Frank's diary had been written by Anne Frank herself during the Holocaust.

Even in the face of the overwhelming evidence provided by these tests, many people are still not convinced the diary is real. There are people who are researching the diary's authenticity, and new theories are being presented all the time. Skeptics claim that the noise made by the people living in the annex, no matter how little, would have given them away, considering how many people worked in the warehouse. Also, in a time of economic depression, how were they able to get an abundance of food delivered? These questions and many others are being brought up constantly to try to prove that Anne's diary is a fraud.

Publishing the Short Stories

A book called *Anne Frank's Tales from the Secret Annex* is a collection of the short stories that Anne wrote during the years she was in hiding. These tales include diary entries, short stories, essays, fables, and even an unfinished novel. They show the range of Anne Frank's development as a writer. They also involve themes that preoccupied Anne in all of her writing: themes such as personal identity in the world, self-esteem and self-love, how to reconcile the way you see yourself with the way that others see you, love of nature and of God, and the necessity of self-reliance. Some of the short stories are titled "Kathy," "Eve's Dream," and "The Flower Girl." The essay

"Why," which ends the book, can be taken as a summary of Anne's short life.

Many of the main characters in these stories are young women in difficult situations. The characters show the same wisdom, idealism, and resourcefulness in dealing with trouble that Anne herself showed. For example, in the fable "Eve's Dream," a girl is taken by an elf into a beautiful garden. There she learns a lesson about beauty and pride from listening to the elf talk about the "behavior" of a beautiful, proud, spoiled rose. Eve is a very smart little girl. She realizes that it may be better to be like the bluebell, a pretty, cheerful flower whose bell swings in the wind to make music for all, than be like the proud rose, whose beauty makes her live only for the admiration of others.

6. Anne Frank and Other Holocaust Victims Remembered

The story of Anne Frank's life is just as compelling, for many people, as her writing. Many have been inspired by Anne Frank; her words have shaped the thoughts, writings, and artwork of artists and politicians worldwide. Even Nelson Mandela, the first black president of South Africa and former political prisoner, used a quote from Anne Frank's diary during one of his speeches.

The Diary of Anne Frank: The Play

The play *The Diary of Anne Frank,* was written by Albert Hackett and Frances Goodrich. It won the Pulitzer Prize and a Tony Award in

1956. Those are two of the biggest honors a play can receive.

Although many people loved the play, there was some criticism surrounding it. Some people felt that the play downplayed the harsh realities of what the Nazis did during World War II. They felt that Otto Frank, during his editing of Anne's diary, had cleaned up the story. By the time the play got to the stage, some people felt it had lost much of its historical authenticity. People said the play concentrated too narrowly on the drama of eight people cooped up in a small space. They felt that ending the play with Anne's words, "I still believe that people are basically good at heart" was an optimistic ending that was unfitting for a play about such a tragedy as the Holocaust.

After appearing on Broadway for the first time, *The Diary of Anne Frank* was seen in productions all over the world. It received strong reactions from everyone who saw it. In Germany, the audience's response was particularly moving.

Liesl Frank Mittler, a literary agent who had arranged for the play to be shown in seven German cities in October 1956, remembered, "At the end of the play, both Berlin and Dusseldorf audiences had the same reaction. The people left in silence, too moved to applaud, too gripped by the terrifying truth of the play's message."

As recently as 1997, *The Diary of Anne Frank* was performed on Broadway. Natalie Portman, known for playing a range of characters onscreen, was chosen to play in the 1997–98 production. The playwright Wendy Kesselman reworked *The Diary of Anne Frank* to include the material that Otto Frank had originally suppressed from the first edition of Anne's diary.

The Diary of Anne Frank: The Film

The film version of *The Diary of Anne Frank* was released in 1959. Frances Goodrich and Albert Hackett wrote the screenplay, which they adapted from their play. The film received eight Academy Award nominations, and won three: Best Supporting Actress (Shelley Winters), Best Cinematography, and Best Art Direction—Set Direction. The sets were, in fact, reproduced exactly from blueprints of the original annex at 263 Prinsengracht.

The same photos of film stars that Anne had taped to the wall in her bedroom in the annex were used on the set of the movie. Dutch glass bottles lined the shelves of the medicine cabinet on the set. The furniture was borrowed from someone who had been a member of the Dutch underground during the war. Even the bread used on the set was provided by a Dutch-American bakery that the film crew found in California.

George Stevens, the film's director, made part of the set on something called spring bedding, which is not as flat and stable as regular bedding. He did this so that during some scenes, the bedding would shake, as though bombs were falling nearby. This mirrors many entries in Anne's diary of how she and the other annex hideaways were terrified by the frequent air raids.

In a feature story written during the filming of *The Diary of Anne Frank* for *The New York Times Magazine*, George Stevens wrote that he had been a lieutenant colonel with a special army motion picture unit during World War II. His unit was with the U.S. troops that freed Dachau, one of the most infamous of the Nazi concentration camps. Stevens did not want to talk specifically about what he had seen in Dachau. He said, "It is something I will never forget." He also said, "It's strange. The voices that dominated Europe for years were those of Hitler and Goebbels, and yet the voice that persists today is Anne's."

Anne Frank: A New Biography

Austrian biographer Melissa Müller wrote a biography of Anne Frank that included the notorious pages that Otto Frank had withheld. It was published in 1998. Müller wanted this to be a biography for adults. In a 1998 interview, Müller said that up until that time, most of the books written about Anne Frank had been geared for teens: " . . . this is, to my knowledge—and I really did a lot of research—the first biography that addresses grown-up readers as well . . . There was no real biography which tries to connect Anne with her family history . . . "

Müller conducted many interviews with Anne's surviving friends and family members. The biography took a new approach to understanding Anne Frank, analyzing Anne's personality within the context of her family history and her relationships with family members, most notably her relationship with her mother. It is a distinctly modern approach to look at someone's family environment when analyzing his or her personality. Because this is the approach that Müller took, many readers feel that her book is a complete portrait of the girl whose diary left them wanting to know more about her life.

Anne Frank: The Traveling Exhibit

The traveling exhibit, Anne Frank: A History for Today, first opened in 1985. It is sponsored and organized by the Anne Frank Center USA. It toured all over the United States for eleven years. It visited 131 communities and had nearly four million visitors. An updated version of the exhibit first opened in 1998. The exhibit continues to visit communities in the United States, educating people about Anne Frank. You can arrange to have the exhibit visit your school. Log on to the Anne Frank Center USA Web site, http://www.annefrank.com, for more information.

People continue to be inspired by the Anne Frank exhibit. As a result, new information about Anne Frank is being discovered all the time. One of Anne's neighbors in Amsterdam,

Edward Silverberg, who lived in New Jersey in 1998, was inspired by the exhibition when he saw it in New York City's Rockefeller Center (sponsored by The Anne Frank Institute of Lower Manhattan). He wanted to talk about his boyhood and about his feelings for Anne. By doing so, he broke a silence of more than fifty years.

Silverberg said, "Anne was different than other girls. She had a lot to say, a lot of very strong opinions. You could have interesting conversations with her. We used to take long walks and we talked a lot." He and Anne remained friends right up until the time that she and her family went into hiding. He was put on a truck that would have carried him to his death, but he jumped off and hid until the end of the war.

Anne Frank Organizations

There are many organizations worldwide that are dedicated to preserving the memory of Anne

Frank. In doing so, they also help to preserve the memory of all of the Holocaust victims.

The Anne Frank House museum in Amsterdam is located in the annex where the Frank family hid. Everything is preserved the way it was left by the inhabitants of the annex. The Anne Frank House is dedicated to educating people about the horror of the Holocaust and the dangers of prejudice, using Anne Frank to put a face to the tragic fate that Anne shared with millions of Jews and other victims during World War II.

The Anne Frank Fonds in Basel, Switzerland, is a foundation that was established by Otto Frank in 1963. The purpose of the foundation is to promote charity work and to serve the cause of peace. Otto Frank especially wanted the foundation to work for the promotion of religious tolerance. The Anne Frank Zentrum is the partnership organization in Germany for the Anne Frank Fonds in Switzerland.

The Anne Frank Educational Trust in the United Kingdom is a sister organization of the

A statue of Anne Frank stands in Amsterdam, Netherlands.

Anne Frank House in Amsterdam. It was started in 1991. Among the many activities of this organization are arranging travel exhibits to bring Anne Frank's story to all parts of Great Britain and presenting educational materials to schools. In 1993, the organization sponsored an event called Anne Frank: Children to Children Appeal, which was a letter-writing campaign that linked thousands of British schoolchildren with children in Bosnia.

The Holocaust Victims Remembered

The Nuremberg Trials were held in Nuremberg, Germany, in 1946. During these trials, Nazi war criminals were questioned about their activities during World War II. Depending on the evidence presented and the testimony of those on trial, some of these people were sent to prison or executed for crimes against humanity.

Many people believe, however, that the Nuremberg Trials didn't do nearly enough to make sure that people are kept aware of the horror of the Holocaust. For this reason, many organizations have been established in many countries to document the events of the Holocaust. These organizations present the information in every imaginable way.

In the United States alone, there is the United States Holocaust Memorial Museum in Washington, DC; the Candles Holocaust Museum in Terre Haute, Indiana; the Holocaust Memorial Center in Michigan; and The Center for Holocaust, Genocide, and Peace Studies at the University of Nevada in Reno. There are also Holocaust museums in Texas and Florida.

Not all Holocaust victims were Jewish. Adolf Hitler's philosophy of an Aryan nation did not include the many different kinds of human beings there are on Earth. It included just one type—the Aryan race. Hitler believed that the Aryans were a master race consisting of non-Jewish Caucasians that were genetically superior to any other race. Therefore, anyone whom Hitler thought was racially inferior, including many Polish citizens and people from Hungary, Czechoslovakia, the Soviet Union, Italy, France, and other European countries, was killed. This included Gypsies, blacks, and homosexuals.

Many organizations that fight racism have been set up in the United States and other countries. These groups are important for many reasons, not least of which is the fact that there is still hate mongering going on in the world. Neo-Nazi groups are still out there, promoting messages of hate and religious intolerance.

Anne Frank's Impact on the World

Anne Frank's honest, touching diary entries gave a voice and a face to millions of Holocaust victims. She has become a symbol of the Holocaust, and part of her legacy has been the foundations and educational programs that promote the cause of peace in the world. As terrible an event as the Holocaust was, Anne Frank's writing ensures that the necessity of remembering it cannot be undervalued or overlooked. This sentiment was best expressed by former president John F. Kennedy: "From the many who stood up for the dignity of humans in times of deep sorrow and big losses, no voice is more urgent than Anne Frank's."

Timeline

1889   Otto Frank, Anne's father, is born in
                  Frankfurt am Main, Germany.

1900   Edith Holländer, Anne's mother, is
                  born in Aachen, Germany.

1914–1918   Otto Frank serves in the German army
                  during World War I.

1925   Anne's parents marry and settle
                  in Frankfurt.

1929   Anne Frank is born on June 12, 1929,
                  in Frankfurt am Main, Germany.

1933   Adolf Hitler becomes chancellor
                  of Germany.

                  The Frank family immigrates
                  to Amsterdam.

1934   Anne begins school in Amsterdam.

1935   The Nuremberg Laws are passed,
                  depriving Jews of German citizenship.

1938   Jewish passports must be marked
                  with a "J."

1939   Germany invades Poland, which sets off World War II. Jews are forced to move to ghettos in Poland, such as in Krakow and Warsaw.

1940   In May, the German army invades Holland and five days later the German occupation begins.

1941   Deportation of Holland's Jews to concentration camps begins.

1942   The Nazis begin the Final Solution.

On June 12, Anne receives a diary for her thirteenth birthday. In July, her sister Margot receives a letter telling her to report to a work camp.

In July, the Frank family goes into hiding in Amsterdam.

1944   On August 1, Anne Frank writes her last diary entry before the family is arrested by the Nazis on August 4.

In September, Anne and the others in the annex are sent to Auschwitz. In October, Anne and Margot are sent to Bergen-Belsen.

1945   In January, Edith Frank dies of starvation in Auschwitz. In March, Margot dies of typhus in Bergen-Belsen. In April, Anne dies of typhus in Bergen-Belsen.

Glossary

annex
An extra section added on to a building.

anti-Semitism
Hatred of Jews. One of the prime causes of the rise
of the Nazis and the Holocaust. Unfortunately,
anti-Semitism has a long history throughout
the world and remains a problem to this day.

Aryan
A word used in Nazi philosophy to mean non-
Jewish Caucasian people with Nordic features
such as blonde hair and blue eyes.

BBC
The British Broadcasting Corporation.

chancellor
The person who is the highest political authority
in a country.

concentration camp

General term for special prison compounds used
    by Nazis and overseen by the SS. Jews, political
    prisoners, prisoners of war, gypsies, and
    homosexuals were among those imprisoned or
    killed in such camps.

death camp

General term for concentration camps devoted
    to immediate mass murder of Jews and
    other prisoners. Also known as
    extermination camps.

emigrate

To leave one's home and move to another country.

Final Solution

The phrase adopted by the Nazi government for
    the plan to kill all Jews in Europe. Sometimes
    historians use "Final Solution" to note the
    contrast with earlier Nazi thinking, which may
    have allowed for "merely" removing Jews from
    Europe rather than killing all of them. The
    removal of the Jews was sometimes called
    "Madagascar," since the island nation was the
    supposed destination.

Führer

German word for "leader"; Hitler's title while he
    was dictator of Germany.

genocide
The mass killing of a group or race of people.

ghetto
A general term for any area of a city set aside for certain ethnic groups of people. Jews lived in ghettos throughout much of Europe. Laws restricting ghettos and activities there have varied greatly over time. During World War II, the Germans established ghettos in occupied countries. The ghettos were intended to help prepare for the elimination of Jews.

Holocaust
Term adopted by historians to describe the mass extermination and murder of Jews by the Nazis. Estimates on the exact number of jews killed vary, but a common number used is six million Jews. Many non-Jews also lost their lives as part of the Nazi campaign to rid Europe of "subhumans."

labor camps
Concentration camps where there were no facilities on site for the extermination of Jews, but where Jews and other prisoners were forced to do difficult work.

Nazis
General term for Germans and others who followed Hitler. Specifically, Nazis were

members of the National Socialist German Workers' Party (NSDAP), which Hitler led. The party was founded immediately after World War I. Hitler took it over in the early 1920s.

propaganda
The use of information, such as words, thoughts, pictures, or speeches, to convince people of a system of thought or an idea.

refugee
One who flees his or her country to escape persecution.

scapegoat
A person or a group of people that is blamed for everything that goes wrong.

SS
The *Schutzstaffel,* or guard unit of the Nazi Party. Members swore personal allegiance to Adolf Hitler. This massive organization swelled to more than one million members during the war. The SS included the Gestapo, the *einsatzkommandos,* and units that oversaw and guarded the concentration camps.

Star of David
A six-pointed star often used as a religious symbol by Jews. Nazi laws required Jews to wear a Star

of David as identification at all times in the
occupied territories, and later in Germany.

transit camp

Camps where Jews and other prisoners were
gathered temporarily before being transferred
to either labor camps or death camps.

typhus

A disease that is transmitted by lice and that is
marked by a high fever and delirium.

For More Information

Documentaries

Anne Frank Remembered (1996). Documentary film that includes interviews with women who were childhood friends of Anne and also with women who were in Westerbork, Auschwitz, and Bergen-Belsen with Anne and Margot.

The Holocaust—In Memory of Millions (1993). Documentary overview of the Holocaust, narrated by Walter Cronkite.

Night and Fog (1955). Classic documentary by director Alain Resnais, considered among the best films on the Holocaust. Subtitled.

Survivors (1999). A Shoah Foundation CD-ROM hosted by Leonardo DiCaprio and Winona Ryder.

Web Sites

Anne Frank Center USA
http://www.annefrank.com

Anne Frank House
http://www.channels.nl/amsterdam/annefran.html

The Anne Frank Internet Guide
http://www-th.phys.rug.nl/~ma/annefrank.html

Canadian Jewish Congress
http://www.cjc.ca/hol.htm

Canadian Race Relations Foundation
http://www.crr.ca

History Place, Holocaust Timeline
http://www.historyplace.com/worldwar2/
    holocaust/timeline.html

Holocaust History Project
http://www.holocaust-history.org

Museum of Tolerance
http://www.wiesenthal.com/mot

The Nizkor Project (Dedicated to Holocaust victims)
http://www.nizkor.org

For Further Reading

Ayer, Eleanor. *The United States Holocaust Memorial Museum: America Keeps the Memory Alive.* New York: Dillon Press, 1994.

Bauer, Yehuda, and Nili Keren. *A History of the Holocaust.* Rev. ed. New York: Franklin Watts, 2001.

Bernbaum, Israel. *My Brother's Keeper: The Holocaust Through the Eyes of an Artist.* New York: Putnam, 1985.

Byers, Ann. *The Holocaust Overview.* Springfield, NJ: Enslow Publishers, 1998.

Frank, Anne. *Anne Frank's Tales from the Secret Annex.* New York: Bantam Doubleday Dell Publishing Group, 1994.

Frank, Anne. *Anne Frank: The Diary of a Young Girl.* New York: Pocket Books, 1999.

Gies, Miep, and Alison Leslie Gold. *Anne Frank Remembered: The Story of the Woman Who Helped to Hide the Frank Family.* New York: Simon and Schuster, 1987.

Lindwer, Willy. *The Last Seven Months of Anne Frank.* New York: Anchor Books, 1992.

Meltzer, Milton. *Never to Forget: The Jews of the Holocaust.* New York: Harper and Row, 1976.

Verhoeven, Rian, and Ruud van der Rol. *Anne Frank: Beyond the Diary: A Photographic Remembrance.* New York: Viking, 1993.

Wiesel, Elie. *Night.* New York: Bantam, 1998.

Index

Index

Credits

About the Author

Magdalena Alagna is a writer and an editor living in New York City.

Photo Credits

Series Design

Cindy Williamson